Welcome to
MALAYSIA

Gareth Stevens Publishing
A WORLD ALMANAC EDUCATION GROUP COMPANY

Written by
GRACE PUNDYK

Edited by
MELVIN NEO

Edited in USA by
DOROTHY L. GIBBS

Designed by
GEOSLYN LIM

Picture research by
SUSAN JANE MANUEL

First published in North America in 2004 by
Gareth Stevens Publishing
A World Almanac Education Group Company
330 West Olive Street, Suite 100
Milwaukee, Wisconsin 53212 USA

Please visit our web site at
www.garethstevens.com
For a free color catalog describing
Gareth Stevens Publishing's list of high-quality
books and multimedia programs,
call 1-800-542-2595 (USA) or
1-800-387-3178 (Canada).
Gareth Stevens Publishing's fax: (414) 332-3567.

© **TIMES MEDIA PRIVATE LIMITED 2004**
Originated and designed by
Times Editions
An imprint of Times Media Private Limited
A member of the Times Publishing Group
Times Centre, 1 New Industrial Road
Singapore 536196
http://www.timesone.com.sg/te

Library of Congress Cataloging-in-Publication Data
Pundyk, Grace.
Welcome to Malaysia / by Grace Pundyk.
p. cm. — (Welcome to my country)
Summary: An overview of the geography, history,
government, economy, people, and culture of Malaysia.
Includes bibliographical references and index.
ISBN 0-8368-2560-8 (lib. bdg.)
1. Malaysia — Juvenile literature. [1. Malaysia.]
I. Title. II. Series.
DS592.P87   2004
959.5—dc22   2003054366

Printed in Singapore

1 2 3 4 5 6 7 8 9 08 07 06 05 04

PICTURE CREDITS
Agence France Presse: 15 (center),
    15 (bottom)
ANA Press Agency: 30
Arkib Negara Malaysia: 15 (top)
Art Directors & TRIP Photo Library: 3 (top),
    6, 8 (top), 12, 16, 20, 31, 39, 40 (both)
Bes Stock: 4, 5, 17
HBL Network Photo Agency: 3 (center),
    7, 8 (bottom), 14, 19, 26 (top), 27, 28,
    34, 35, 37, 38, 45
International Photobank: 1, 23, 26 (bottom),
    33, 41
John R. Jones: 21
Earl Kowall: 2, 11, 18, 22, 32, 36
Lonely Planet Images: 9
Malaysia Tourism Promotion Board: cover
David Portnoy: 24, 25
Sarawak Museum: 10
Shaw Organisation: 3 (bottom)
Times Editions: 13, 29

Digital Scanning by Digital Colour Works Pte Ltd

Contents

5   **Welcome to Malaysia!**

6   **The Land**

10 **History**

16 **Government
and the Economy**

20 **People and Lifestyle**

28 **Language**

30 **Arts**

34 **Leisure**

40 **Food**

42 **Map**

44 **Quick Facts**

46 **Glossary**

47 **Books, Videos, Web Sites**

48 **Index**

Words that appear in the glossary are printed in **boldface** type the first time they occur in the text.

Welcome to Malaysia!

Malaysia is a land of modern cities and ancient rain forests. The country has a colorful heritage that includes many races, traditions, religions, and cultures. Let's visit tropical Malaysia and learn about its history and people.

Opposite: Flying kites is a popular hobby in Malaysia.

Below: Malay boys usually wear plain cotton shirts. Islam teaches that clothes should be clean and not too colorful.

The Flag of Malaysia

The Malaysian flag's fourteen red and white stripes and fourteen-point star represent the country's thirteen states and the capital city of Kuala Lumpur. The **crescent** is a symbol of Islam. Yellow is the royal color of Malaysia.

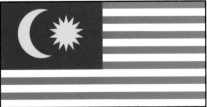

The Land

The country of Malaysia has two parts, which, combined, have a land area of 127,317 square miles (329,751 square kilometers). **Peninsular** Malaysia lies between Thailand, to the north, and Singapore, to the south. East Malaysia is 400 miles (644 km) across the South China Sea, on the island of Borneo.

Left: This *Orang Asli* (OH-rahng AS-lee) village is in the lush green hills of northwestern Pahang, which is part of Peninsular Malaysia.

The Banjaran Titiwangsa mountain range runs from north to south along more than half the length of Peninsular Malaysia. The land south of this range is fairly flat. Along the coasts, many small islands surround the peninsula.

East Malaysia has many mountains, and, at 13,455 feet (4,101 meters), Mount Kinabalu, in the state of Sabah, is Southeast Asia's highest peak. The country's longest river, the Rajang, is also in East Malaysia.

Above: Many of the tropical islands off Malaysia's coasts have beautiful coral reefs. They are also popular places for swimming, diving, snorkeling, and windsurfing.

Left: The trunks of many of the trees in Malaysia's rain forests have huge **buttress roots** to hold them up. Because of all the heavy rainfall, the soil of the forest floor is very thin.

Climate

In tropical Malaysia's hot and **humid** climate, temperatures average about 80° Fahrenheit (27° Celsius) all year round, except in the mountains. The highland areas are much cooler.

The country has only two seasons. The dry season starts in May and ends in September. The rainy season lasts from November to March.

Below: The colorful rhinoceros hornbill is one of more than 350 kinds of birds in Malaysia.

Plants and Animals

More than twenty thousand kinds of plants grow in Malaysia's rain forests. Some of them can be found only in Malaysia. One of the most spectacular is the rafflesia. This plant has no leaves or stems, but its flowers are huge.

Tigers, leopards, rhinoceroses, and orangutans are some of the many kinds of animals that live in the rain forests. The variety of marine life in the waters surrounding Malaysia includes whale sharks, giant leatherback turtles, and all kinds of tropical fish.

Left: The rafflesia flower grows only in the rain forests of Malaysia. With blossoms as big as 39 inches (99 centimeters) across, it is the largest flower in the world.

History

Prehistoric tools discovered in Perak and Kelantan and human bones found in Sarawak, some possibly dating back to 35,000 B.C., are the only remaining signs of Malaysia's early history.

The Malaccan empire, which began in the fifteenth century, was one of the first important Malay kingdoms. It was founded at Melaka, along Malaysia's southwestern coast, by a prince named Parameswara. Melaka quickly became a prosperous trading port for Chinese, Malay, Indian, and Arab merchants.

Left:
The bones of some of Malaysia's early human inhabitants were discovered in a cave in Sarawak, along with these paintings on the cave's walls.

Left:
To protect Melaka against attacks, the Portuguese built a huge fortress, called A'Famosa. Today, only a small part of the fortress is still standing.

Colonial Rule

In 1511, Portugal conquered Melaka. Under Portuguese rule, trade suffered and steadily declined, even after the Dutch took control in 1641. In 1824, Melaka became a British colony. With British developments in agriculture and tin mining, conditions improved.

Forming a Federation

By the 1900s, Britain ruled Malaya, which consisted of nine states in what is now Peninsular Malaysia. In 1942, during World War II, the Japanese took control of Malaya and ruled until 1945.

When Japan lost the war, the British returned to Malaya and tried to set up a government that decreased the power of Malay leaders and gave equal rights to citizens of all races. Malays saw this government as a **threat** to their rights as **indigenous** people and, in 1948, formed the **Federation** of Malaya.

Left: St. George's Church is a well-known landmark in Penang. Built by the British in 1818, it is the oldest Anglican church in Malaysia.

Independence

In the Federation, Malay leaders kept their power, but Britain still controlled the country. Fighting for independence, Malaya's three main **ethnic** groups, the Malays, the Chinese, and the Indians, joined their political parties to form a union called the Alliance. Winning an election held in 1955, the Alliance took control of the government, and in 1957, Malaya declared its independence.

Above:
Tunku Abdul Rahman (*far left, with arm raised*) was the leader of the Alliance and became Malaya's first prime minister. At a ceremony held on August 31, 1957, he announced the end of British rule.

Modern History

When Singapore, Sabah, and Sarawak joined the Federation in 1963, Malaya became Malaysia. Singapore withdrew, however, in 1965. Malaysia struggled during the 1960s, especially with racial problems. The nation's New Economic Policy in the 1970s and twenty years of strong leadership under Prime Minister Mahathir bin Mohamad improved both social and economic conditions.

Left: This statue, called the National Monument, is in the Lake Gardens in Kuala Lumpur, Malaysia's capital. It was created by Felix de Weldon, an American sculptor.

Tunku Abdul Rahman (1903–1990)

Considered the father of independent Malaysia, Tunku Abdul Rahman had a strong belief in national unity. He played a key role in freeing Malaya from British rule and was the country's first prime minister (1957–1970).

Tunku Abdul Rahman

Chandra Muzaffar (1947–)

In 1999, Chandra Muzaffar lost his job as a professor at the University of Malaya because of his political beliefs and human rights activities. Today, he works with international organizations and leaders to promote world peace and to end discrimination.

Chandra Muzaffar

Marina Mahathir (1957–)

The oldest daughter of Malaysia's fourth prime minister, Dr. Mahathir bin Mohamad, Marina Mahathir has received many awards for her AIDS-related community service.

Marina Mahathir

Government and the Economy

Malaysia is a federation made up of thirteen states and three territories. The federation is ruled by a **constitutional monarchy**. The position of monarch, or king, however, is only **ceremonial**. The power to govern Malaysia belongs to **Parliament** and an appointed prime minister. The prime minister is usually the leader of the political party with the most representatives in Parliament.

Left: This modern building in Kuala Lumpur, Malaysia's capital city, is called Parliament House. It is home to both the Senate and House of Representatives, which are the two governing bodies that form Malaysia's Parliament.

Left: During World War II, the Japanese used this British colonial building in Johor Bahru as a fortress. Today, it is the State Secretariat Building, which houses a variety of government offices.

Local Government

In addition to Malaysia's central and state governments, large cities have councils that are responsible for local **facilities**, and rural villages elect their own leaders to rule on local matters.

Left: Rubber is made from latex, which is a milky white liquid that comes from rubber trees. The process of collecting latex from the rubber trees is called rubber tapping.

Economy

Until the 1970s, the most important industry in Malaysia was agriculture, and the country's main **export** was rubber. Today, many of Malaysia's exports are manufactured products from a variety of industries, including electronics, automobiles, and steel.

Malaysia's industries attract many foreign **investors**. One reason for so much foreign interest is the country's industrial free zone, which allows its manufactured products to be exported without a lot of **customs** paperwork.

Cottage Industries

Small companies that manufacture handicrafts, local food products, and other items that are usually sold only in local markets are called "cottage industries." These industries are a very important part of Malaysia's economy and are valuable sources of income, especially in rural areas. Some of the cottage industries in Malaysia are now also exporting their products, which include wood carvings, handwoven baskets, and *batik* (bah-TEEK).

Left: The Proton car company is Malaysia's leading manufacturer of automobiles. This Proton automobile has just come off the assembly line at a Proton factory in Shah Alam.

People and Lifestyle

About 58 percent of Malaysia's people are ethnic Malays. These indigenous people are known as *bumiputera* (boo-mih-poo-TRAH) and include the group Orang Asli, which is believed to have been the country's earliest inhabitants. All other ethnic groups are referred to as "non-bumiputera." The two main groups of non-bumiputera Malaysians are the Chinese and the Indians.

Below: Because of its location at the center of the main eastern trading routes, Malaysia's population is a mixture of many different cultures and ethnic groups.

East Malaysia

Many different groups of indigenous Malays live in East Malaysia. Some of these groups still practice traditional customs and live by hunting, fishing, and farming. Because East Malaysia is less developed than the peninsula, more of its people are extremely poor. In some places, entire villages live under one roof, in **longhouses**.

Family Life

Marriage and family are highly valued in Malaysia, especially among Muslims and Buddhists. Until nearly the end of the 1900s, divorce was very rare.

In Malaysian families, children, parents, grandparents, and even great-grandparents often live together in the same household, and younger members of the family typically turn to the older members for advice and guidance.

Left: Because they are inexpensive to buy and to operate, motorcycles are a common form of transportation in Malaysia, especially for people with low incomes. Often, a motorcycle is the only transportation for an entire family.

Left: Many families living in Malaysia's rural areas have five or more children. In the cities, however, largely because of the higher cost of living, many families prefer to have only one or two children.

In most families, men and women have traditional roles. Men are usually the main wage earners. Women are usually homemakers. Today, however, with more women going on to higher education and entering the workforce, traditional roles are changing.

Children are taught to respect adults but are also encouraged to speak their minds, as long as they do it respectfully and do not lose their tempers.

Education

Malaysian children can begin preschool at the age of four or five and can stay in preschool for up to three years. At age six or seven, they go to primary school. Secondary school starts at age thirteen.

Secondary education is divided into three levels. After completing lower secondary school, students must pass an exam to go on to middle secondary. The exam taken at the end of middle secondary school determines whether a student moves on to pre-university studies or to **vocational** training.

Left: Many schools in Malaysia offer classes that teach computer skills. Along with required subjects such as English, history, mathematics, and science, secondary students can also choose courses in industrial arts, agriculture, and foreign languages.

At all levels of education, most Malaysian schools teach classes in the Malay language, called *Bahasa Melayu* (bah-HAH-sah MUH-lah-yoo). A few schools use Chinese, English, or Tamil, which is an Indian language. Students in all schools, however, are required to learn English and may choose to study Chinese and other foreign languages.

Instead of going to national schools, some Malaysian children attend private schools that offer instruction based on the Islamic religion. Malaysia's private Islamic schools are called *madrasahs* (mah-DRAH-sahs).

Religion

Islam is Malaysia's official religion, and most Malay people are Muslims, but the country's many ethnic groups also practice other religions. Most of Malaysia's Chinese are Buddhist or Taoist. Indians are mainly Hindus or Sikhs. Some Chinese, Indians, and Eurasians are Christians. Many of the indigenous Malays in East Malaysia are also Christians.

Above:
When Muslims pray, they face the city of Mecca, in Saudi Arabia. Mecca is where the prophet Muhammad, Islam's founder, was born.

Left: Instead of worshiping at a church or a temple, a Muslim prays at a mosque. Ubudiah Mosque, in Kuala Kangsar, is one of Malaysia's most beautiful mosques.

Left:
These Buddhists have gathered at a temple in Melaka to pray. As an offering to the gods, they are burning long sticks of sweet-smelling incense, called joss sticks.

Each religion has its own beliefs and **rituals**. Muslims are required to pray five times a day and are not allowed to eat pork. Buddhist worshipers burn joss sticks as an offering when they pray. Hindus believe that they will die and be reborn as a different being, again and again, until they finally unite with God.

Language

Although Bahasa Melayu is Malaysia's official language, the population speaks a variety of languages. Mandarin is a common language among the country's Chinese people, and Tamil is the most popular Indian language. Malaysia's more than sixty groups of bumiputeras, or indigenous people, each have their own languages, too. The oldest of these groups, the Orang Asli, have several languages which, as a group, are called *Aslian* (AS-lee-an) languages.

Left: Poetry is a respected form of literature in Malaysia. These young girls are participating in a primary school poetry recital.

Left: This stone, which is called the "Inscribed Stone of Terengganu," dates back to the 1300s. The lettering on it is the earliest known Malay writing.

Literature

One of the most important pieces of Malaysian literature is *Sejarah Melayu,* which is the first recorded history of Malaysia. It was written by Tun Sri Lanang who lived during the time of the Malaccan empire.

Today, A. Samad Said (1935–) is one of Malaysia's best-known writers. Originally a journalist, Said later wrote poetry, short stories, plays, and novels. His famous novel *Salina* tells how the country suffered under Japanese rule.

Arts

Most Malaysian art is based on religion and culture. Malay architecture and paintings have Islamic **motifs**. Chinese sculptures and paintings reflect nature and Chinese beliefs. Sculptures of Hindu gods decorate Indian temples.

Below: Traditionally, batik fabrics were made by hand. Today, machines are often used to produce batik's brightly colored patterns.

Traditional Crafts

Batik, wood carving, **pewter** and silver work, and weaving are all traditional Malaysian crafts. Handwoven products include household items, such as mats and baskets, as well as hats and other articles of clothing.

Opposite: This woman is weaving traditional Iban clothing. The Iban are the most well-known indigenous group living in the state of Sarawak.

Dance

Since ancient times, dancing has been one of Malaysia's most important art forms. Although the ancient dances are rarely performed today, theatrical and modern dance styles are very popular, and the ethnic groups of East Malaysia each have their own dance forms.

Mak yong (MACK yawng) is one of the most popular types of theatrical dance. With its combination of ballet, opera, comedy, and romantic drama, a mak yong performance usually has to be stretched out over five nights.

Architecture

Most older buildings in Malaysia are a mixture of colonial architecture and Islamic style, and older cities still have many shophouses that were built in the early 1900s. A shophouse's two-story design allowed a business owner to live and work in the same building.

New buildings have modern designs but also include Islamic features. Kuala Lumpur's Petronas Towers, currently considered the world's tallest building, are shaped like eight-pointed stars, which symbolizes the spread of Islam.

Above:
This building has walls of woven bamboo, and it was constructed without nails. Once the palace of the sultan of Perak, it is now the Perak Royal Museum.

Leisure

Malaysians enjoy both traditional and modern activities. Flying kites, spinning tops, and an indoor game called **congkak** (CHONG-kak) are some of the most popular traditional pastimes. For people living in the larger towns and cities of Malaysia, movies are a favorite modern way to spend leisure time.

Below: Because they have crescent-shaped tails, these colorful kites are called *wau bulan* (WOW BOO-lan), or moon kites.

Contests and Tournaments

Kite flying requires a lot of strength and skill. Traditional Malaysian kites are up to 12 feet (4 meters) long! Kite-flying contests in Malaysia are very popular events. They include both local and foreign participants and kites of all colors, shapes, and sizes. The winning kite is judged on its design as well as on how high it can fly.

Malaysia's top-spinning tournaments also attract contestants from all over the world. The person who throws the top that spins the longest is the winner.

Sports

The most popular sports in Malaysia are the kinds that can be played almost anywhere, without much equipment. For Malaysians, these sports include soccer, badminton, and *sepak takraw* (seh-PAHK TAHK-raw)

Malaysians love to play soccer and are faithful fans, whether watching it on television or cheering for any of the twenty-four teams in the country's two soccer leagues. Thirteen of these teams go on to play for the Malaysia Cup.

Left:
In both cities and rural communities, soccer is a favorite sport of school-children and Malaysians of almost any age.

Left:
In 1998, Malaysia opened the Sepang F1 Circuit, one of the best Formula One race tracks in the world. Racing in the 2001 Italian Grand Prix, Alex Yoong became Malaysia's first F1 driver.

Badminton has gained much of its popularity in Malaysia since 1992. That year, the nation won the Thomas Cup, which is badminton's highest award.

Sepak takraw is Malaysia's national sport. *Sepak* is a Malay word meaning "kick." *Takraw* means "ball." This fast-paced sport is like volleyball, soccer, and gymnastics rolled into one. Players must pass a ball back and forth across a net — without using their hands!

Holidays and Festivals

Many of the holidays and festivals in Malaysia are religious or cultural celebrations. Regardless of religion or ethnic background, however, most Malaysians take part in all of them.

The biggest Islamic holiday is *Hari Raya Aidilfitri* (HAH-ree RYE-ah ih-dih-FIT-rih). It marks the end of Ramadan, which, for Muslims, is a month of **fasting**. Officially, this national holiday lasts two days, but celebrations usually go on for a week.

Left: To celebrate the Hindu "festival of light," families pray over a special fire to thank a god named Vishnu for defeating a demon that had kept the world in darkness.

Left: Colorful lion dances are part of many Chinese festivals, including Chinese New Year. People believe that these dances bring wealth, luck, and long life.

Most Chinese festivals are noisy celebrations that include parades and fireworks. On the eve of Chinese New Year, families gather for a feast, and at midnight, fireworks light up the sky. Although Chinese New Year is a three-day holiday, festivities last fifteen days.

Deepavali (dee-PAH-vah-lee) is a Hindu holiday. Known also as "festival of light," it celebrates the victory of light over darkness, or good over evil. Indians in Malaysia start the day with family prayers and a special breakfast. Then, guests arrive to visit and to feast.

Food

Besides representing many cultures, Malaysia's ethnic groups also represent many **cuisines**. Today, however, some Malay, Indian, and Chinese dishes are commonly considered Malaysian. They include an Indian dish called *roti canai* (ROH-tee cha-nye), which is a pancake that is eaten with curry, and the Malay dish *nasi lemak* (NAH-see ler-MAHK), which is rice cooked in coconut milk. Rice is a basic food for all Malaysians, and it is eaten at all meals — breakfast, lunch, and dinner.

Above: Street dining and food stalls have been common in Malaysia for a long time, but fast food restaurants such as McDonald's and Burger King are rapidly gaining popularity.

Left: This woman at a food stall in the city of Ipoh is frying banana fritters, a popular snack food in Malaysia.

Malay dishes are generally served with rice, and Malay cooking uses lots of herbs and spices. Beef, chicken, or fish may be included, but Islamic law forbids Muslims to eat pork or anything cooked with pork products.

Although rice is often served with Chinese dishes, noodles are popular, too. Like many other foods in Chinese cooking, noodles are often stir-fried. They are also served in clear soups.

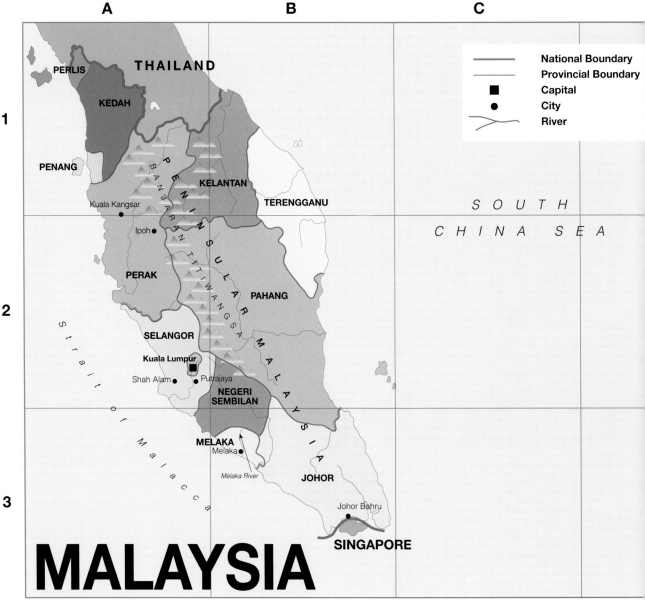

MALAYSIA

Banjaran Titiwangsa
   A1–B2
Borneo D3–G1
Brunei F2

Celebes Sea G2–G3

East Malaysia
   E3–G1

Indonesia D3–G2
Ipoh A2

Johor (state) B3
Johor Bahru B3

Kedah (state) A1
Kelantan (state)
   A1–B1
Kuala Kangsar A1
Kuala Lumpur A2

Labuan F2

Melaka (city) B3

Melaka (state) B3
Melaka River B3
Mount Kinabalu G1

Negeri Sembilan
   (state) B2–B3

Pahang (state)
   A2–B3
Penang (state) A1
Peninsular Malaysia
   A1–B3

Perak (state) A1–A2
Perlis (state) A1
Putrajaya A2

Rajang River E3–F3

Sabah (state)
   F2–G1
Sarawak (state)
   D3–F2
Selangor (state) A2
Shah Alam A2

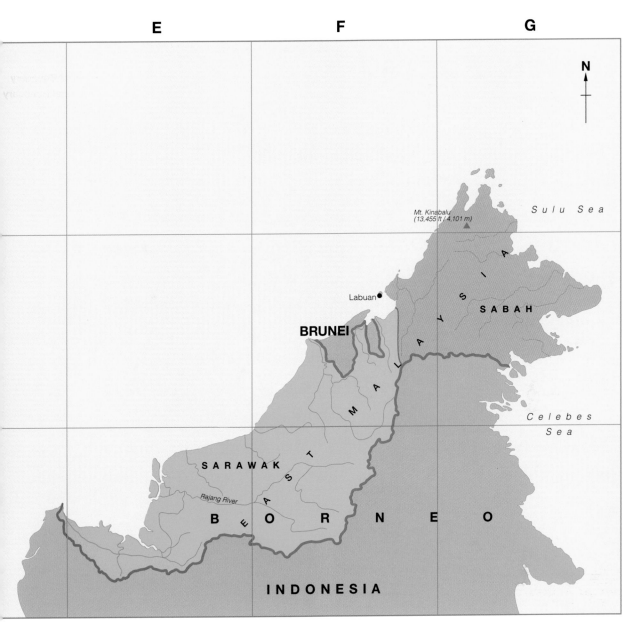

Singapore B3
South China Sea
   B3–G1
Strait of Malacca
   A2–B3
Sulu Sea G1

Terengganu (state)
   B1–B2
Thailand A1

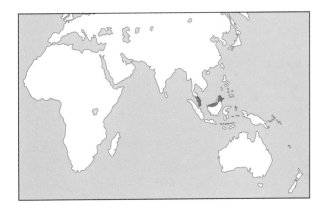

Quick Facts

Official Name	Malaysia
Capital	Kuala Lumpur
Official Language	Bahasa Melayu
Population	22,662,365 (May 2003 estimate)
Land Area	127,317 square miles (329,750 square km)
States	Johor, Kedah, Kelantan, Melaka, Negeri Sembilan, Pahang, Penang, Perak, Perlis, Sabah, Sarawak, Selangor, Terengganu
Federal Territories	Kuala Lumpur, Labuan, Putrajaya
Highest Point	Mount Kinabalu 13,455 feet (4,101 m)
Longest River	Rajang 350 miles (563 km)
Major Religions	Islam, Buddhism, Hinduism, Christianity
Important Holidays	Chinese New Year (January/February)
	Wesak Day (May)
	National Day (August 31)
	Deepavali (October/November)
	Christmas (December 25)
	Hari Raya Aidilfitri (varies on the lunar calendar)
Currency	Malaysian Ringgit (MYR 3.8 = U.S. $1 in 2003)

Opposite: This dancer is wearing a colorful costume to participate in a National Day parade.

Glossary

batik (bah-TEEK): patterned fabric made by waxing and dyeing cloth.

buttress roots: wide roots projecting outward and upward on a tree's trunk to provide extra support in thin soil.

ceremonial: honoring a tradition.

congkak (CHONG-kak): a two-person game of strategy played on a boat-shaped piece of wood that has cuplike hollows containing marbles, shells, stones, or seeds used as counters.

constitutional monarchy: a type of government that is led by a king or a queen but is ruled according to the laws of an established constitution.

crescent: a thin, curved moon shape.

cuisines: specialized styles of preparing and cooking foods.

customs: the fees that must be paid on goods brought in from other countries.

ethnic: related to a group of people from a particular country or culture.

export (n): a product sent out of a country to be sold in another country.

facilities: services and conveniences.

fasting: not eating at certain times or for certain periods of time, especially for religious reasons.

federation: a group of separate states or nations that have united under a central government.

humid: damp, usually describing the amount of moisture in the air.

indigenous: belonging to a country's original, or native, people.

investors: people who loan money to a business, expecting to receive a share of the profits or earnings.

longhouses: very long, one-story wooden structures built on stilts that traditionally house an entire village of native people in East Malaysia.

motifs: patterns or designs that follow a theme and are usually repeated.

parliament: an official government body of elected representatives who make the laws of their country.

peninsular: located on a strip of land surrounded by water on three sides.

pewter: a type of metal that is usually a combination of tin and lead.

rituals: ceremonies and practices.

threat: something that might cause harm or loss.

vocational: related to an occupation, profession, or skilled trade.

More Books to Read

Abdullah's Butterfly. Janine Fraser (HarperCollins Australia)

Chopsticks for My Noodle Soup: Eliza's Life in Malaysia. Susan E. Goodman (Millbrook Press)

Kuala Lumpur: A Sketchbook. Chen Voon Fee and Kon Yit Chin (Tuttle)

Malaysia. Ask About Asia series. Allen Roberts (Mason Crest)

Malaysia in Pictures. Visual Geography series. Lerner Geography Department (Lerner Publications)

The Petronas Twin Towers: World's Tallest Buildings. Record-Breaking Structures series. Mark Thomas (PowerKids Press)

A Photographic Guide to Birds of Peninsular Malaysia and Singapore. G. W. H. Davison and Chew Yen Fook (Chelsea Green)

Southern and Eastern Asia. The World in Maps series. Martyn Bramwell (Lerner Publications)

Videos

Mystical Malaysia: Land of Harmony (Questar)

People of the Rainforest. Rainforest for Children series. (Schlessinger Media)

The Pilot Guide to Malaysia & Southern Thailand (Library Video)

Web Sites

abcmalaysia.com

travelforkids.com/Funtodo/Malaysia/ malaysia.htm

www.geographia.com/malaysia

www.nationalgeographic.com/ earthpulse/rainforest/

Due to the dynamic nature of the Internet, some web sites stay current longer than others. To find additional web sites, use a reliable search engine with one or more of the following keywords to help you locate information about Malaysia. Keywords: *batik, Kinabalu, Kuala Lumpur, Mahathir, Petronas Towers, Sabah, Sarawak.*

Index

agriculture 11, 18, 24
animals 8, 9
architecture 30, 33
arts 24, 30, 32

badminton 36, 37
Banjaran Titiwangsa 7
batik 19, 30
Borneo 6
British 11, 12, 13, 15, 17
Buddhists 22, 26, 27

Chandra Muzaffar 15
children 22, 23, 24, 25
Chinese 10, 13, 20, 25, 26,
    28, 30, 39, 40, 41
Christians 26
climate 8
crafts 19, 30

dance 32, 39

East Malaysia 6, 7, 21,
    26, 32
economy 14, 16, 18, 19
education 23, 24, 25
ethnic groups 13, 20, 26,
    32, 38

families 22, 23, 38, 39
festivals 38, 39
flag 5
food 19, 21, 40, 41
Formula One (F1)
    racing 37

government 12, 13, 16,
    17, 25

Hindus 26, 27, 30, 38, 39
holidays 38, 39

Iban 30
independence 13, 15
Indians 10, 13, 20, 26, 28,
    30, 39, 40
industries 18, 19
Ipoh 40
Islam 5, 25, 26, 30, 33, 38
islands 6, 7

Japanese 12, 17, 29
Johor Bahru 17

Kelantan 10
kites 5, 34, 35
Kuala Kangsar 26
Kuala Lumpur 5, 14, 16, 33

language 25, 28
leisure 34
literature 28, 29
longhouses 21

Mahathir bin Mohamad
    14, 15
Malaya 12, 13, 14, 15
Malays 10, 12, 13, 20, 21,
    26, 40, 41
Marina Mahathir 15
Melaka 10, 11, 27
Mount Kinabalu 7
mountains 7, 8
Muslims 22, 26, 27, 38, 41

Orang Asli 6, 20, 28

Pahang 6
Parameswara, Prince 10
Penang 12
Peninsular Malaysia 6, 7,
    12, 21
Perak 10, 33
Petronas Towers 33
plants 9
Portuguese 11
Proton cars 19

rafflesia 9
rain forests 5, 8, 9
Rajang River 7
religion 5, 25, 26, 27,
    30, 38
rice 40, 41
rivers 7
rubber 18

Sabah 7, 14, 21
Sarawak 10, 14, 30
sepak takraw 36, 37
Shah Alam 19
shophouses 33
Singapore 6, 14
soccer 36, 37
South China Sea 6
sports 36, 37

Thailand 6
top spinning 34, 35
transportation 22
Tunku Abdul Rahman
    13, 15

women 21, 23, 40
World War II 12, 17